SEA and FOG

OTHER TITLES BY ETEL ADNAN

ETEL ADNAN

SEA and FOG

NIGHTBOAT BOOKS

CALLICOON, NEW YORK

SEA

to Simone Fattal

The sea. Nothing else. Walls ruptured. Sea. Water tumbling. Oil. Transparency. The sea. Field of stirring liquid. Gathering of pouncing waves going to battle. Into one's mythology, trees intrude, expand, shed shadows.

A wave, a mouth; a horse arrives, submits, drowns. Streaked and bleeding sky. What is sky? To climb mountain peaks to overlook clouds. Water on water reverberates memory's mechanism.

Oh fire's explosion from a woman's gut! Organized fearful battalions on the march. Soldiers cover their eyes with flowers, given the season. Continents of drifting clouds on the move.

Sea insomniac with jealousy, sky moving eastward. White foam covers the water. Disquieting silence. Matter's feminine essence surging as sea's quiddity.

Rain falls. Fire-spirits create clamor and thirst in the audience. Can water be thirsty? While thunder gathers energy lines of waves turn into musical scores. Thinking captures the sounds and throws them into the storm.

The sea ignores Achilles' death and can't be warned, as we have forgotten her alphabet. Space narrows down to a slit: radiation reaches the brain, burns neurons. Sliding into deep sleep, the brain erases all, cancels itself.

In an invented summer the world breaks apart. Slowly, mountains appear... through a multitude of traps set by divinities. Are these beings still among us? Sometimes they are.

For lack of essential audacity, we value misdeeds. Eyes remain riveted on the moon that's rising from the edge of a man's sorrow.

Infinity's presencing – going against the monsoon. Winds sweep the imagination while the spirit dries up. Small memories drift away. The brain – soft bag – collapses on itself. Stripped speech patterns float in the soul's canyons where things are perennial.

Dryness peels away the soul caught in gravity's unconquerable solitude. The body's magnetized metals turn naturally North. The face, with eyes, mouth and nostrils, strains to remember intricate mental constructions. Bones end dust over dust.

Death withdraws from the plains that lead to the sea. The latter turns me into a mass of beneficial water where the heavy bird of heat tests its wings. I'm letting go. The entering fog is eager for human presence. Not a stranger, not a pause.

The spherical ocean's luminescence is a thing familiar, but our energies won't respond to its call; they're designed for the body's penetration by salt, and the soft happiness that invades the spirit when water meets light.

To take leave from the moon and go in deeper night. On its other side, to encounter Being. Spiritual fields of attraction. Immateriality.

The hour returned to renewed landscape. A piece of paper disintegrated, and water engulfed an Egyptian deity. But what is Egypt for the sea? Or Syria? They, lands of the accumulated ferocious secretions that we name history, for lack of a better word.

I have not seen war, by being in it, and missed the Pacific's advancing pyramidal waves by living nearby. Love went astray, an animal, a wind.

Some people give their lives for a boat, others would rather swim. And what about the corpses that sharks feast on? Did the belief in resurrection rise from the repetition of the kind of innocence that water induces in the body?

Late afternoon. Such apprehension, such madness! Is the sea aware that her heroic beauty may be in disuse, someday? The moon never experienced the sinking of empires that she witnessed; day after day, she longs for a shimmering heat.

As for you, you will not hear but spin around your own axis, cross your limbs within a circle; the dizzying sense of immortality will floor you and make you find and lose what you had already lost and kept.

Water's iridescence is language. An exchange of blood endangers our arteries for this salt, this oil. A privilege. Brown stains line the sea as she furiously breaks herself against the coast's tormented rocks. 'I', lighthouse waiting for storms.

The sea's instincts collaborate with ours to create thinking. Our thoughts come and go, in birth and evanescence. We feel we own them but we're the ones to belong to the radiations that they are, lighter than fog, but endearing in their unreliability...

Massive clouds break up to uncover other skies where no divine order betrays its existence. Waves are gentle with the sun's early rays. Traces of melted copper line the shore. We will not die.

Sea's Passion. Ophelia no longer woman, Medea submerged in blood. Luminous beams shed light on the humiliation. The sea has no arms to uplift the sky. Planets are forbidden islands, still forbidden.

Elemental sounds. Always alive, this seamless livid creature. But what is life? A scintillation? On a clear day a different kind of clarity starts to be lacking. We face the river.

O these walls that surge, building impregnable fortresses, then collapse suddenly, in fierce light, and rise further down, in similar though not similar repetition.

And this erratic edge called restless tide changes its geometry, and with urgent, terrifying power, covers the flat rocky formations that were here and are no more, when waters and foam are so icy that the spine calls for mercy.

Towards the evening, there's pain, turbulence, fever. Cafés remain open. Currents circulate freely. The Sea of Cortes has exact knowledge. Its fire is subsumed as water. An encounter with it can happen anytime, as the heat would be there.

Nothing is grounded. Large stretches of land cover secret mobility. Underground floods erupt, expressing anger. The world is essentially mute. In the obscurity of one's brain the ocean roars a triumph.

The sea is not having nightmares about the Milky Way. Coppery clouds descend through a passage down to the coast. The hills loom in a steely blue color that can slay the heart by its beauty.

We're spending a life loving it exclusively because we couldn't change the world. Blinded by its light, our retinas rest on its epidermis, follow its ripples. Its assaults are mercurial, its nights, impenetrable. Voices speak of a species which is wounded. Space is not some abstract notion but our own dimension.

Matter calls for matter, unfolding on hypnotic territory, oozing from the belly though remaining indifferent. It keeps us outside its absolute privacy. So where do we stand? We can drown in it, be dissolved, forgotten.

Like autumn leaves, my thoughts fall on paper. The ocean is near, the sea, far.

Insinuating itself between cuts and bruises, its ubiquity makes of water a divine substance.

Geometry's ecstatic powers overtake the mind. Geometries undefined. Not an apology for perfection, nor an alternative notion of form, but the fusion of sounds with light, there, where anything goes wild within change's archaic identity.

She was friendly, that morning, in the midst of catastrophe, her breathing regular. She had diverted us from our fate. Death was pacing around but didn't touch her. There was life to her life.

Once in a while comets befriend boats. In their inability to cope with reality, passengers attribute this experience to hallucination. Fish follow the cruiser.

Soon, disoriented but keeping full speed, a body intact throws itself against demented waters; the two masses, the single spear-like and the oceanic other meet, clash, then fuse their weight in an ultimate reckoning with Being.

But where are the trees, the trembling trees? Meadows in Middle America are on the alert. Wingless creatures, they dream of killer whales. Winds have stirred the tide; that blue surface is arching its back. The moon has reached fullness.

With unceasing movements the sea, having missed her cohesion, returns. The center is about loss. Far from separation or unity. Loss as the price for Being. Being is mind's obscure horizon. An incurable presence seduces us with no possibility left for escape.

A monument enters through the window. The sea is childhood's sole companion, it says. To understand her – or any object, mental or material – one has to increase one's surrounding obscurity to a breaking point. We're standing within a hypnotic affinity with history.

And what is this surge of the stupendous and quasi un-nameable entity, where un-numbered amounts of bubbles unbreakably bound to each other make a eulogy for smallness while creating the most maddening form of an elusive infinity?

Measure beyond measure, we shift to discover a longing that pulls us toward the universe's destiny.

Thus waves come in pairs.

.

Love is wedded to time, and revelation is their breaking apart. In one of August's sizzling days, the sea swallowed a woman whose flesh gave up resistance. Funerals did not take place; instead, the sea howled all night long.

I laid epic tales on her undulations to quiet down her belly's turbulent monsters. She desired to keep her tides frozen because of her unspent love for the night. Directions vanished under a breeze possessed by a tempest.

In its eruptive solitude no volcano approximates the forces unleashed by angelic mutations. Would her phosphorescence deeply penetrate my fabric? Modulations of light faster than speech, than thought, arrest the brain. Where's the water of disappeared rivers?

Light is attuned to fury. In mirrors, always exhilarating. Our senses are made of its stuff, non-codified, insomniac. We love its turmoil; winds carry dust to it, and to the ocean; more water, element of insanity. O astonishing immateriality of distances!

Sea, made of instants chained. Where to shelter impermanence within its defenses? A threat, for sure. What about the permanent affinity between light and mind, both a processing machine, of particles, of thoughts?

Strong pulls are felt toward one's fate: the mountain's pulse leads to the voyage's openness.

The horizon asks not to be pursued. We can't figure out what was whistling all night long, having lost our deed of ownership for the sky. Ghosts stand as sentinels of past loves. Nature doesn't deal with the past; nowadays, uncertainty skims its waters.

At times, the sea unleashes its daemons. Gods remind her that they laid on her surface their earliest writings though these fell into her abyss. People threw roses and the flowers perished. Children were used in obscure sacrificial rites.

Death drove fast through a black forest. Signs pointed to disaster. Destiny behaved soft, terrified. Waves got transformed into decapitated gelatinous bodies. In the shallows, temperatures fell. Growths are curtailing the daylight. Despair is running free.

Bodies produce words among other secretions. Stretched sails. New entities. Wings hover over charged particles. Streams are heading toward an approaching night; currents en route to some wedding.

America's immensity doomed by language's fall. Ocean bounded. Illumination and death, non-comparable twins. We're exasperated by water's alarming coherence. Theories are disarmed by the sky's curvature. What remains closed, distant, foreign, will feed new thinking.

Not ever hesitating, waves surge to reach human speech. They propose a truce. When we forget Ahab and converse only with Moby-Dick, the universe will manifest itself in full clarity.

And the sea ceased to be because it became the sea, and we stopped at the station of impermanence, and rose from our bewilderment to witness the junction of the past with the present.

We stood at the beginning, the sea's rhythm found its momentum and progress was made. The fire had no smoke. It was apocalyptic. It smelled of algae, of phosphorescence. A trumpet blows in every light-ray. An emperor's head is rolling in blood.

Disquieting messages keep pouring from destiny. We borrow energy from unlikely sources. One side of the mind tells that everything is gray, the other is a speedboat. The two hemispheres have a hard time connecting.

Mountain peaks breach a regal order to hear divine talk. Sea and light are not chartered. On the contrary, they are defiant, as they have always been. Ulysses and Dante are ghosts, not dust.

Fog reigns supreme. It descends like Chinese rivers, envelops water and land. At times, it weighs, adds itself as hills on hills. What should we forego to recover kinship with the weather?

Sky is pale. Its sorcery lays one low. Far below, warriors blame it for their predicament. Its transparency is a burden, they say. Its anteriority defeats them. They had invested in power, not in the pleasure of their agility.

Sea: mirrored mirror that distracts the soul from ecstasy. The uncontrollable desire to think the fleeting elements of the world, to fuse them into images, into words, is probably the most hypnotic of all of Eros' manifestations.

Morning. Vast. Imprecision. Fog has covered everything in gray absolute. This has lasted. Doubt looms over the mind. Absence is harder to accept than death.

Darkness was put into orbit and Creation skipped its laws. Ever since, we move in confusion.

A drop of water plus a drop of light have arrived before language, in Being's pristine isolation.

In strange though tormented flights, wind runs from Alaska to North Beach, north of the Bay. Sands are waiting, fish worrying.

Deep is the night when storms hit the sky's dimensions. How extended is the spirit over Being's unfathomable extension!

The heart pounds for desire. Questions remain unanswered in tropical heat. No leap backward to Mayan temples.

Look well at the Pacific before you die. The best of the promised paradises have neither its hues nor its splendor.

.

Autumns slide along rivers in a haze. On solid ground, a woman turns her back to the day's last moments. Something non-human, immaterial, is calling her spirit.

When the universe thinks itself without being outside itself, we name that "thinking" God.

By landing on the moon, Neil Armstrong made a widower of our imagination. Since, we sail with no embarkation. Nature's fatigue brings pain to the sun's eye, mud to the Scriptures. The rain dispersed the mountain.

Mornings, shaper of bodies, stretch the view. How to not dread black holes and their turbulence! Only waves on waves, that's what's coming. I want to go insane, said the sea. She will.

Universe and sea made an agreement: the one provides substance and the other, movement. But suddenly, within time's thickness, sea worries. Her movements are reduced. Is Orion angry? She returns to water, an element she trusts.

It was late afternoon. The children had played in and out the waters, then the sun came down to join them, now an extinguished balloon. They kicked and laughed and tore that toy apart. During the night they dreamed of a sea that was their mother.

Phantasmagoric, she governs our wildest desires. We try to get by where there's only drought. We deliver salt to illicit love affairs and dizziness brings havoc to our mental powers. There has never been land under my feet.

Who's cut off from the invisible? The sea is momentous duration. A passion for her is love for an illusion. But what else is there to be had?

An angel blows his tuba in the sky's lights, blowing his head off. Clouds are torn-up. Here on Earth, we rescue – from deep waters – sunken vessels. The spirit shrinks in front of a horse's black speed.

The massive weight of liquid space intrudes into my sleeplessness; bears heavily on my creaking bed. That expanse is insomniac by essence and I, by fate.

Shadows settle in the eyes of those who look at the sea. There's glory to the body's form. Hiding in your rage, o my Euphrates still not properly named, from Asia's high peaks, into the Gulf and the expectant ocean, you run to become my own odyssey.

Before water appeared on its surface Earth was burning lava. The divine is not spatial but needs space, is not material but needs matter, is not human but needs consciousness, is not a work of beauty but needs the sea's power of attraction.

What will happen to the waters when Earth will fall apart? An over-population of angels wants to escape from heaven because east from here there are valleys illuminated... and further east the sea whirls around its islands and holds them either as presents or prisoners...

A new millennium is a tidal wave of future history. We'll see the forming of new languages, the disappearance of familiar things, rats, canaries, bulls... there will be psychic phenomena running loose.

This is this. This is that. In between, existence's duration, our efforts of understanding. In the meantime, the pine makes a shadow on the oak tree; the image reaches the brain in spite of myriads of exploding suns. Electronic flowers unfold into sentences of doom.

I'm transported to the ocean's most intimate core. Light falls on an eerie world! While caves suck in my metallic and winged body, rockets take off, I say. Whales swallow pieces of fallen stars. Large estuaries open up to the sun.

Flowers do cry. They sense danger but their weapons can't keep predators at bay. It rained then we witnessed the unfolding of a panoply of rainbows. Standing as an elephant among us, what did the carnivorous ocean do if not devour Caesar, Hannibal and Moby-Dick?

The heart's tightening coincides with the sea's dilation. Valleys are filled to the rim with snow. What can one do with the possibility of uprooting the forest, seeding the waves with uncertainty? Our load of melancholy has no itinerary. Why should it?

'It' is not an animal. Not glass. Not a pencil, not a wall. Not an eraser. 'It' is not a reflection or some iron, a fuse or a curtain. Not some water in a bottle. Not a jacket, a door or a floor. Not a lamp. Neither eatable, nor perishable. Not to be approached by negatives. "It" is endless.

Two pygmy sperm whales, a mother and her calf, got stranded in south New Zealand on a sand bar slightly out to sea. A bottlenose dolphin flew to their rescue, led them 200 yards along the beach and through a channel out to the open waters.

Confronting invisible beings such as spirits behind sealed doors creates non manageable terror. A snowy peak in Montana is contemplating a flight of vultures over the lower elevations. I see a series of rivers lying side by side with no barriers between them. Land and fire.

Soldiers are shooting at each other but there's no trace of the color red under my eyelids, only a purplish curtain, stirring. Annihilation lurks in the distance. On this occasion, the sea's double is my own mind. They asked: is the sea woman? I said yes.

I used to chase the sun that was rolling in the sky and shining in puddles – in Beirut's young streets. Later, I read that not far from Luxor, they excavated brains dried and in perfect condition. Archeologists smashed them to decode their DNA. This crime spoiled my day.

Without a body there's no soul and without the latter there's no way to speak about the sea. A guy was contemplating her when suddenly he was seized with panic. He started to change shape, to melt. His descent was hard, perilous. She didn't help him.

And then the next page, wave or airplane. Constellations take the contour of our thoughts, and scatter them right and left. There's this path, narrower than a foot that leads to the ocean.

In Space's obscurity our eyes, created by the sun, fail us. They share the fate of our organs which are resigned to living in darkness. During some storms, we perceive, in lightning, elements of a supreme intelligence.

.

What does it mean to be water? Can I comprehend you in ignoring intelligence, and contain your immensity? When the cold freezes you, it slows down my blood. Under the moon's attraction you rise and fall as my mind vacillates and fails.

You have to divorce the sun for having flooded the labyrinth and dissolving Ariadne's bones. You betrayed the shores of the islands that you locked in battle with you. Who are you, you my shadow's watery shadow?

Some young men claim descent from the stars; others fear a nuclear meltdown. They live with the anguish of being at creation's beginning. High temperatures. The soul's garden is planted with roses. The horse race is over.

The brain heats up and distorts the world to squeeze out new meaning, and lets the sea proceed with her other lives. Light springs from the night. We absorb its incandescence. Water by water reflected, desire by desire burned, stretch time's skin to unforeseeable receiving ends.

She thundered, turned over herself. Fish panicked. The news alerted the coral reefs. Later, her calmness was even more scary.

In between there was Greece and Rome, but Rome's gods, unlike Greece's, seem to have departed for good.

Matter's mutation into velocity is its guarded secret. So we barely scan surfaces while we think that we're penetrating mysteries; we consider dust to be pulverized mountains, and luminous rays, Being's manifestations...the sea swallows fire just to prove her freedom.

Distances are better defined by birds' flights. No spirit was haunting the water. No defeat. Matter had not solidified. There was neither knowledge nor a knower. No impatience. The wind was not moving yet, no it wasn't. Movement hadn't yet needed to move.

God is not dead. He's ultimate terror. God is everything, it's said. Therefore He's the sphere unbreakable, the all-knower, it's said. Therefore, there's nothing left to be known. He could be absolute darkness or absolute light; it comes to the same. God is born out of the fear of pain, decay, or disappearance. That fear is the experience of termination, the all-encompassing gap that renders time meaningless.

God guarantees eternal life and is loved for it. But eternity is death's favorite name. Only consciousness is life, a reality that is the awareness of the passing of things, and that itself passes away. God being eternity can only sink within Himself.

But the universe is alive, so how can its parts die? Still, we die. Some will say that we don't die, but change. So God who doesn't change is a kind of death, an ominous one. We can't rely on that. And the promised paradise, in its immobility, is death too. If life comes out of death and returns to it then God watches candles be lit and then extinguished.

The sky fell and storms blew on its face. It sank deeper; in that maelstrom humans lost balance. There were fires on earth and questioning in the waters.

And why is it that sea is the sole element that dream can't transform? Its translucency remains intact in the dark, in lustrous innocence.

So life is a dream infinitely less gripping than the one we visit in sleep, less dangerous.

Is the I of the dream the one we frequent in daytime? It uses languages we ignore, has capabilities otherwise unreachable, time-sequences which open up some of Nature's locks.

In those turbulent nights I swim through many large, torrential and merging rivers, that disorient their own speed and storm out of space, to take me into new perceptions with exhilaration and awe.

Between Earth and outer space there's a passage whose transgression brings transfiguration. We're propelled away from our usual condition. Our cities' avenues confront those of the imagination. The world in shambles.

The past stands behind our shoulders, always instantaneous. We can't calm a tempest with a slash of the sword. We wonder: has Orpheus ever walked under the sea's floor? I suspect he remained in the light's richness.

Abrupt falls, a fall. Gravity is pulling us in. Light runs – like mother to child – to embrace this moving surface caught in its sameness. Water and light create that shimmering which takes our breath away.

Like Medea, she belongs to mythology: she hurls herself against her reefs. She's boiling, boiling, convulsing in light's undulations, surging and falling with buoyancy against the surrounding heights. For seeing the sea it's sometimes better to close one's eyes.

Ocean is first child of Sky and Earth, while Time is the last. It spits menacing waves and restructures itself, an eruption of a special kind. A beast.

The starting point of infinity is always at the center, where mind resides. Behind an image there's the image. Nothingness is Being's foundation, put on stage by poetry, which makes the erotic and the intellect meet. It's not life, it's alive.

Trees are meant to stay erect. They spread their branches for the duration of their lives; they shed their scales/leaves, withstand a storm while the sea falls back on its horizontality.

With banners unfurled, she turns kingdoms into fields of algae and corals; with a heredity of sacred prostitution, she transforms whales into peaceful monarchs; from her pregnant belly rise cities of flamboyance inhabited by crepuscular visions.

In her factories where fish are used as slave labor, she manufactures languages. In fire, in anger, Earth trembles at its progeny's fury, knowing that in the end matter will send the spirit reeling.

Waves pound the coast the way blood infuriates the heart. Through time, the moon accumulates prerogatives. The man who is lying there, not wearing trousers, not eating sandwiches, has established friendship with that planet on its own terms, the way numbers follow laws which are not of their making.

There's sea, ocean, and turbulent rivers, and there are the Great Lakes, matrix of storms, last refuge for mythologies, sailing ports and platforms for interstellar voyages. The Lakes: beauty's perennial domain! Silent or in turmoil, iced or fluid, unstoppable, they slide into their own under innumerable galaxies.

We try to abandon the world to itself. Dionysus recurs in full independence from anything pertaining to the Pantheon. It's a pristine day over the many mountains and their torrents.

A cosmology of terror: History's recurrent theme of tortured bodies dumped as garbage. The sea commits incest regularly with primordial violence and fanfare. She moos. We believe in the uniqueness of these times as in the originality of this sky. The tribe needs to.

That mass for which we have only one or two names determines innumerable lives. It's beyond the realm of doubts. It's fully given and, still, a maddening mystery. We sleep eye to eye with it, but by then it's invisible.

Everything goes through trial by water in a constant here-ness. Nothing to dread. Let's walk and run, go to the beach then to another beach, and then take a swim, take a boat, ride a whale.

A young woman is a bride and the groom doesn't always belong to the human species. The day's first rays make a crown for her. Space is made of layers, like a rose, like a cake. It provides room for her, and much more.

The horizon's perfection is due to its virtual reality. Alone in the midst of waves, the spirit pushes ahead. The horse and the vessel claim the same god.

Everything is surface on surface, light on light, being on being. We face the aggressiveness of rocks biting with futility at the surf's mercurial flesh. Memory will use anything, now that we left the sun far behind.

Ignoring its obscure side, the soul rushes into this clarity; we call it a crossing of transparencies. This particular moment is mediated by a draft of air.

If from so much afar you remember me, send a sign. I used to walk through flowered gardens down in streets with barely discernable figures; in full sun I was moving fast, accompanied by orange trees. Carried by this feast, I was reaching your shores, and, removing my clothes, I was softly going in, sliding toward your waters and swimming.

There are places within the mind where messengers deposit dreadful news. The Merced River hurries to wash out the mane of evil that covers our heads. We carry our memories in backpacks. The fog's lightness surprises the senses, until the foghorn blows its complaint. The heart beats evenly.

Often there's no discernible shoreline. Air evolves in darkness and sounds keep distant pitch. Primordial chaos yearns to fade away in colloquial invisibility. At times, in fog, in blackness, one dreams of coming creations.

An uninterrupted series of fallen empires descends nightly on my soul. Birds perform one more flight when they turn their attention to the Bay's luminescence. After a while, the wateriness of the water becomes something of the past.

The sea is to be seen. See the sea. Wait. Do not hurry. Do not run to her. Wait, she says. Or I say. See the sea. Look at her using your eyes. Open them, those eyes that will close one day when you won't be standing. You will be flat, like her, but she will be alive. Therefore look at her while you can. Let your eyes tire and burn. Let them suffer. Keep them open like one does at midday. Don't worry. Other eyes within will take over and go on seeing her. They will not search for forms nor seek divine presence. They will rather continue to see water which stirs and shouts, becomes ice in the North, vapor in the tropics.

Salt glimmers on the lover's body. Lingers. Tears return when heartbreaks don't heal with time. The sea ushers old games of passion and release.

There was a wave which lost its way and found a tree. There were questions in the air. These two awkward creatures were not by their education prepared to meet. The one could have drowned in the other. The wave could have had its brow broken. But they fell in love and since, the sea is green and the forest is blue.

Nevertheless, pink flamingoes walk by the edge of men's dreams who envy the shimmering light that these birds radiate. Further on, there's more light and a call for a further flight.

And the mirrors are waiting to fill their void, and the remote sea thinks that her tempests will never be taken in consideration by that counter-world where happens only that which happens simultaneously elsewhere. Then where to go?

It's before the reaching of words that thinking is at its most telling: an electrical wave haunted by meaning and moving on the brain's surface like God's spirit trembling on the meeting waters of the Tigris and the Euphrates. At its source, neither material nor spiritual.

Dawn always strikes with stupor. That's the hour when, before committing suicide, Mayakovski scribbled his last words: "Lili, love me!"

Eyes have busied themselves exclusively with seeing although they can hear better than ears whenever they join forces with what's outside the mind's perimeter.

With phenomenal perversity the sea enters fissures, transforms the body into a sieve. Skins turn into rotten leather and eyes fall as if they were fruits from trees exposed too long to bad weather.

Within seconds, X rays and gamma rays have hit us at light speed. A cloud of nuclear particles at 5 million miles an hour engulfs everybody's brain. We are monitoring the universe in real time.

Latest news: and who framed the universe, who and for whom? I created it for the sake of clouds, and all the stars behind. For light's light. For the sea, to be.

Yes. As everyone who heard of Melville knows this oft repeated remark: "meditation and water are wedded forever."

The need to forget pain but not its origin. To approach that which is most hidden, our inner organs. The day you will penetrate your brain, what a mess won't you find! A dump yard! God may be found in there, too, in the brain's brain that's involved with the creation of artificial intelligences.

Mind has its own technologies; poetry is one, but it eludes total comprehension. Open the window, let air in. The sky is now a rubbery orange-colored fluff, and the ocean behind me, a child's tempest.

Something as immaterial as space brings relief. I haven't vented my anger, haven't dried my mouth, haven't sent the letters that still need to be written, and haven't spent sleepless nights with a lover, so what is this uninterrupted process that makes me aware of all this?

With hesitant steps, I entered a circle of oak trees and was asked to shed my thoughts, which I did. Surfers do not interfere with our wars. Bloodshed won't bring them any reward.

Let your back lie on the water and be a raft for birds, then in the middle of the night, dive. Your ears will ring, spit fire; the waters will remember that once they were you.

Elements. Elemental. Before the original cell there was a will, and still before, a name. There was wind and, before, animated powers. The power was divine and divinity tangible. Chaos exploded and left a sound behind, still heard, still feared.

And we are here, anywhere, so long as space would be. Is given to us sea/ocean, sea permanent revelation; open revelation of itself, to itself. Mind approximates those lit lines in the front, that darkness above, meant not to understand but to penetrate, to silence itself while heightening its power, to reach vision in essential unknowing.

The sun hasn't set and there's no light. O the obscure clarity out of which we are made.

Light graces pugnacious waves. Through my eyes, it looks at galaxies. Having escaped the sun's inferno, it turns into angelic substance and reflects upon its own nature.

To what are we destined? It's getting cold. Hurricanes are devastating the land. Night has descended. It's sucking the years to come as it did the former ones. Time is a utopia. It leaves no residue on our hands.

They project running contests of fabulous storms. The mind is keeping up with the hullabaloo and it's useless to hurry given that history has no radical closure.

A tournament of feathers conscripted against words. The foghorn blows in all directions then the clouds lift the fog. What we see: a throne descending. Its essence is temptation. We lose reference. It's superfluous to wait, a new order of things having settled.

They say that furniture perspires when nobody's around, but all we have is funereal immobility. The world has been inventoried. Father and horse belong to the past. How to tell Dionysus that his face is deformed by the fire that he feeds?

The great slaughters consistently perpetrated throughout history are jamming the conduits to the sea, claiming anonymity. She washes carefully the humiliated bodies thrown to her, before annihilating them in the oblivion she harbors.

A massive storm joins the voyage, there, where voyager and trail fuse. How mercurial is Being! Implying continuity, History is a metaphysical concept: the sea, its outer skin, the body, its seat, war, its energy.

Humanity is an ocean, each person a bubble, appearing, disappearing, and reappearing on its turn.

The fog's independence speaks for Nature's intelligence. Light is dimmed for the ocean to divide. The Golden Gate sways. Everything is freezing. We have been eaten by a killer wave so long ago that we speak from its belly with no inkling of our past or future misery.

As we decompose with no remission, wounds flatten. Blowing winds mix bits of brains with dry leaves and arteries turn into hallucinatory sewers. The mind reels on the internet, churns ideas as if they were weather events, and electric shocks awake the prisoner in the middle of his nightmare.

War-torn African jungles fooled many navigators; stacks of flying equipments were discarded along fetuses, worn up shoes and aged maps. They sent musicians from over there, one shipping at a time.

The mountain is not witnessed although the clouds are absent. Tension is rising and the labyrinth is cacophonous. That's a goat's vision blurred by grass that stands tall.

Marco Polo entered the Indies' red waters with sunken skies on board. Suddenly, Agamemnon surged from a pool of war scenes with metal forayed into his flesh. Perverse sirens bathed him in acid and landed his remains on Crete.

And now, ahead of fear, within eyeshot of the ocean, having followed fate to the bitter end, it won't be enough to say that it was hail and thunder that rained at the center.

This planet seeps into the mind's corridors. Nights are getting cooler. On the avenues' aridity days start on time; the body is memory's privileged subject.

Even when I'm swimming she seems to be at a distance. Her waters feel like an intimate encounter of differences. There's no transgression. We're mesmerized by immensity touching our body, and instead of a prison, being a liberation.

Giordano Bruno was burned at the stake; still, the door opened and he appeared, a canto of sub-particles turning into the lightness of words and bringing a new order to glorify the divine.

Do senses precede the soul? Displacing the question: does life precede birth, precede itself? The spring's youth intensifies meditation. There are rumors about the existence of a new kind of matter. The idea had already occurred to Lucretius but the discovery is recent. A boat down the coast was loaded with fresh news.

She has covered her tattoos with kelp. There's a girl in the bar slightly taller than the billiard board. Sailors stagger toward her, but then, they leave.

I told a tree: be a tree! and it did. It grew and screened its environment. The sea won't listen. Its crust is scaly. The mountain is blanketed but its crest is out, for breathing. If it weren't for the hour there would have not been light. A profusion of it. The abominable threat of war is momentarily lifted.

Yellowthroat, peregrine falcon, sandpiper, egret, blue heron, double-crested cormorant, shorebird, come on, space is yours! Translucent. Uncreated. Free from any of us. There for thereness' sake. Oh the wind's jealousy!

The seeing and the saying: the young spring illuminates alleys lined with green trees. But why say it when it's not up to words to convey a reality of this sort? The vision has already fused with the universe's history. Now, it's gone! The same is true of the sea. To linger can lead to suicide, an experience that eludes narration.

We build on the ephemeral. Following a thyme bush's fragrance, we discover Guernica filled with smoke. Somebody stole the lamp. The war was lost due to compositional failure. Airplanes, stop it! Beatific vision requires elevation. We are engaging you to pay the mortgage on the groom's bed, on the bride's torn little dress.

Look how things stretch beyond their limit! First, one arrives with flashlights, then hears voices. A sand storm is displacing mountains. In their agony, they dream of a farm. Afterwards, the generals will eat human flesh and swell with the bombs that their bellies are sheltering.

A few camels have shown up by the stream. Their enlarged memory-chambers contain images from the war. A soldier on foreign land can't shake off the evil gnawing at his feet. The poor are fearless. They get help from the dead. They will wait long enough for invading armies to age, get married, and die.

This mass of sorrow, this packaging of the heart, this fear running under swift waves, what a defeat! We plunge into an endless night.

And, unleashed, clusters of forces are assailing the Night Palace, the self's fortress; but the latter will withstand their assault until Being's own demise: o enchantment, o confusion!

I see infinite distance between any point and another. That's why time has to be eternal. We went to the moon once under a propitious weather and loved each other in ways we couldn't achieve on our terrestrial habitat. Once in a while, we laughed.

Microwave radiations pour over Earth. They penetrate the brain and transform it into a furnace. The fish dive deep. Islands quiver and rock back and forth. This turmoil brings joy as well as many questions.

Poetry reaches the unsaid, and leaves it unsaid. It's familiar, it's indecently close, overpowering at times, as gray as cloudy skies over melancholy mountain ranges; It's what it is, and for ever the question remains about its nature, and why we're still looking for an answer.

Mermaids misunderstood vileness, and the sea – sheet of brown paper calm and brittle – subdued their voice. She provided surpluses of energy to the land's massive interior. California has a breath of its own. The first man that stared at her must have been baffled by her sheer grandeur. My share of the cosmic brain sees her as incestuous.

We are kept awake by the monsoon's twisted arrogance. The sun is consumed with grief over the soul's lunacy that shines darkly on pools covered with soft leaves. Memory's function is to randomly redistribute the latter on the coming days.

A woman possessed by love unfulfilled haunts the cemetery. Tombs must remain closed even if she needs to open them in search of the passion she lost. Something ancestral stirs in her guts.

There's space, for sure, we're of it, but where's time? Where from? There's change, and it is movement. No doubt. So time, abstracted from change, is movement represented by a watch's needles. The measure of change we call time. As we fear death, a fatal change, we fear its progression in everything. Although we love change and marvel at movement.

Outer space is morally neutral, not a solution. This planet is still friendly so we can embrace some of its lovelier manifestations by letting time bypass our thoughts. But what is that thing that makes us wait for non-events?

Each second may be the last, that's why even stones worry. Old instincts, deeply buried, are resurfacing. Despair is morose. Short-winged rough winds. Sea vomiting corpses. Earth and sea are fighting each other. For the return of the waters.

Clouds are turning into fire-pits devoid of revelation.

Finally, Nietzsche didn't empty the world of its past but, instead, drained his own mind. His brain became an empty shell resonating with his former writings.

Each tear, repressed, returns as a wave; a bus missed, as a storm; a day gone, a sunset. The sea repeats herself, like repeated is one's absence to this world's promise.

Sometimes our thoughts smell of roses. Magnetic waves lord over the waters. There's indolence in the surrounding darkness but spirit-powers, bearer of visions, descend on us. And with the Hudson - while air is mobilized by invisible life - strange currents mix.

What about Earth's durable existence? What will happen to the Niger River when the world will age? Seen from the moon, the earth was water, and it had the colors that we attribute to the sky.

In these times of global over-heat wells are losing their sweetness. The mind uses solar dynamics to sustain its activities. Is matter a transvestite, one asks. We look at childhood from the telescope's other end. Some want the absolute possession of that child, in fear, in shame.

Does a functioning brain taste salt? When continents will turn into steam, will we be still going to where tempests surpass their own momentum? Will we see divinities in their iridescence and be an audience to the explosions of light produced by our disincarnated souls?

To leave in order not to stay. To feel that the self is departing and needs to be followed, to sense that all is happening outside of that thing that doesn't have a center.

The forest is shaking terribly. Waves howl and break in jets of water. What beauty, this fury! Sea: it's because she is that we are, and when she disappears we'll cease to be. It's only in relation to her that we find some worth to our existence.

In this moment, the sky is made of silver. That metallic and cosmic plate deflects light into our brains.

To feel the cold is to fear the falling apart of one's bones.

It promises the Word in no other form than emptiness. Involved with its own becoming, it renews itself within its echo and matter listens. The horizon is not its limit but the sign of its survival. Everything is in peril when morning occurs.

Of all the modes of being, with the help of books, or in any other ways, what is of paramount importance to the mind is what – alas! – will disappear with death: the everyday physical body. Its inherent pleasure to be.

Finally, the crossing of layers of obscurity doesn't guaranty transparency. Hammering one's head against its inner walls doesn't crack open the absolute but rather breaks the spirit. O eternity, to love you to no avail! Not being a whale or a tree, I will find contentment in being the sound of water.

And to Anne Waldman: as if the sea had opened into an alien planet with its own seas, as if we had already gone to a different universe, never resting, as if the sea were the only certitude, incandescence on the mind's shores, apocalyptic silence, as if it were love unconditional for light's appearance next to trees readying their wings.

On Mars expect a kingdom of extremes: minus 100 degrees Celsius at night. A year of 669 days of 24 hrs & 40 minutes. Monsoons on its face. 200 times less ozone than over Earth, 10.000 times more carbon-oxide than on Venus!

The body produces that superstructure we call mind. When they work together there's elation. But they can go – too often – their own ways, the body damaged beyond repair, the mind destroyed beyond recourse. All the while the world manifests its overwhelming power.

Photography is akin to medieval thinking: it values the instant, is based on the microcosm, the atom which mirrors the whole, the DNA which identifies. To see is to arrest the world, to save it from submersion.

The sudden apparition on a page of an Italian pot planted with a miserable little bush is akin to desire's birth, in the fog.

And then a leap. A word, a wave. An agitation from within the skull, migratory migraines having exhausted all theories. The body is pumping grime into the heart. Animal instability keeps luminosity perplexed.

She's youth mixed with algae, contaminated by cells from sunken sailors. Tides ebb and flow while in their beds women swell up with erotic fantasies; they are envying her, having always got some gripe.

I will spread a piece of soft linen, somewhere, and lie, invite a slow air to fill my lungs and return the world to itself... O to be a place with nothing around.

Poland is not Colombia, not Bolivia; not a pool for the former Soviet Union; not Eastern, being west of Mongolia; is a big surface on a map... and that's the way we think.

This synthesis of mineral memories, this matrix, is, of things to come, the mercurial certitude. Its underbelly is distended, malicious, rotten, but the climate takes on the hues of its will.

Stanley "Tookie" Williams requests us, before his death by lethal injection, to remember "Strange Fruit," Lewis Allan's song of 1940:

> Southern trees bear strange fruit
> Blood on the leaves and blood at the root,
> Black bodies swinging in the Southern breeze...

The song was the pure extraction, from Allan's brain, of an incubating idea that was itself withdrawn from its mother's grace, its origin.

And there are these river waves running on insidious territory, this light folded on itself, a line so close that it penetrates the pupils and hits the spirit's heart. As there are no furrows, nothing is planted.

She's a book, at times, whispering in our dormant ears fleeting texts. Does she have a destiny? If by destiny we mean incurable solitude, we can say that she carries Being's structure in ways that escape our understanding. Sea and Being are accomplices.

Then when did thinking start? Did it have something to do with the sea's unfathomable centrality?

What is unique is multiplied; accumulated drops of water create her sovereign self, her colored spots, the sounds she emits, and look at her, sometimes as ominous as the Himalayas, vaporous like Saturn's rings... Destiny is that movement whose sole aim is to continue to move.

Therefore everything rolls and unrolls, runs and misses, weighs and crumbles, is circular and orbital; everything resembles itself in immutable space.

Last words from Van Gogh on his deathbed: "The sadness will last forever." From Heraclitus: "The world is not born from time, but from thought."

Sea: massive energy in sync with mathematics, electric field producer of ideas, in mist, in fog, traveling, erupting in ears, and to eyes, bringing an arrested vision.

Bullets explode in brains as confetti on a holiday celebration. Young men in the ghettos have the freshness of dew. They mistake death for a wedding.

Tumultuous is Being, in agony though not dying. Surrounded by fury. Different in every instance, a stranger to the soul. Where are we in these inter-stellar gardens, at which latitude, in relation to what? Some of us sink into them, others disappear in where stars left traces of burns on the grey envelop of their thoughts.

Within the night, a second night; within a loss, another loss. Which abundance of pain would snuff out memory? Where's the tearing, (not of clothes, not of the body), that will bring out Being's hard core, and break it?

Van Gogh, Louis Armstrong, Gagarin: my friends. In the meantime, astronomers have identified a violent explosion at 50,000 light-years away from Earth. But there are explosions here too, countries disintegrating.

For eyes awakening in a haze of heat, a body's undressing by a herd of admirers is mystic activity. In these cities of perdition a wind mixed with spray clears the head and helps it see Being's inbuilt brutality, the big fires advancing on the mind with great strides.

Yesterday, I went to bed with the sea because I was feeling that we were both structurally alike. She lives off the universe's pulls and pushes, the way, at home, we lived off my mother's beauty.

The oak is green, is a unit. The sea, indivisible, cannot be a number. Fixing one's eyes on it – in bracing weather – is a metaphysical enterprise. The mind, though attracted to that flooding, tries to avoid that apocalyptic encounter.

We carry a lamp in our labyrinthine brain and search for hidden memories. Sparks of former experiences surge at the intersection of past and future, death being the eternal present.

This field of energy streaked with heavy shadows sends light's immensity to our eyes, tiny windows on the universe's depth.

We grew metallic wings. Relinquishing the sweet taste of bathing in the sea, we bring to planetary caves news from Lascaux and the Fezzan Valley.

With suddenness, under an immemorial canopy of shifting clouds, two bodies fuse their heat to create love's birth.

We don't have the means to be this clarity instead of receiving it; but the mind outraces light's speed, throwing this body behind, like it does mountains and planets.

The table and the ocean at this moment share flatness, luminosity. Space opens out from right to left, as it remains open, regardless, having burst the margins of our perception.

We climbed a short distance and on the horizon witnessed a green light left behind by the sun's setting.

.

Withering realities and systems of immortality are rolling and exploding, and nowhere is life warmer than where the sun's age is the Earth's.

O ocean, sending cargoes of jellyfish to corporate dinners, when I say that you were not created do I mean that you created us? Leather replacing one's eyelids cannot be dissolved in high temperatures. When I loved the ocean I was young.

Lost battles look at waves for comfort. Ocean of majesty, offered in my honor, you are the sovereign of our territory and all writings testify your power. When I walk by you I become a third figure, and angels speak – then – of bewilderment, with voices I recognize.

Because you are, and I am, you were, and I was, we shall die – but not disappear.

Faint, harmless, snowballs splash on the fringes of Earth's atmosphere. We'll meet them outside from all we know.

"What if
        when crocus is
              over and the rose
                    beginning"

the moon were to return to the Night Palace? We will then probably live a transfigured mythology.

We have to stitch the Earth together. Our crepuscular fate floats aimlessly. On the beach I pick up words fallen from people's mouth.

Ocean, widowed by the sea, the gods you made became astronauts when the breeze blew them beyond the forbidden gates. In your wild purity – there, where my life has started – under an airplane, you drew currents of pure water, water our present.

Smooth-skinned, a heavenly body lands over a field of irises. It lacks the tranquility that fire requires, although some other form of stillness may coexist with this openness. Unfamiliar forms circulate at odd hours. Does immateriality have to be an obstacle?

Solar winds strip regularly Venus and Mars of their gases. It's always clear skies, over there.

Love buried with the lover's body. Trusted to demented women wearing their shiniest clothes. The ocean is waiting, used to the passage of seasons, having heard goddesses sing. It's suddenly spring. Flowers born overnight.

Being is alive. Life brings life. Being repeats itself, a fact of existence. That repetition we call time because it implies time's existence. What's then reproduced, repeatedly and with no interruption? The answer is: Being itself, the return of the Same, for an eternity of time.

Death is the end of our intuitive knowledge of Being. To say that Being recurs implies that it manifests itself in minds other than one's own. That's what we mean by a reality independent from us.

Scientists say they found heat, fissures, plumes of water, vapor and ice shooting out from Saturn's moon Enceladus. This is the Holy Grail of planetary exploration. We're looking, throughout outer Space, for earth-like environments. We're incapable of facing a dream different from the flatlands we live on.

The 'I' is a frontier; most tenuous of threads. Between what we were a fraction of a second ago, and what's coming, we hang on a filament: our sanity. The transaction makes what we call the self.

A total solar eclipse cast an eerie blue glow across the sky and the sea. It cut a dark swath across the sky. In Iraq, people recite prayers in the mosques out of fear of an additional catastrophe. The moon masked the sun and Venus suddenly appeared. Mayakovski's suicide occurred on April 14TH, 1930.

As if the world would first stop at the edge of the big cities, then penetrate their parks, their houses... Nothing is ours. We are owned by Necessity.

Seamless thinking of seamless matter: the river, abandoned, gets larger as it approaches its favored ocean, sweeping everything on its way. The higher the eye climbs the wider becomes the spirit...

And what if the mind were a well, deep but still with a firm base, though not a material limit? There would be water in there, real water, dark, oily, at turns slimy, that once in a while rebels, overflows; and isn't that cataclysmic event what we name "sea?"

Like a dam of darkened old wine broken loose, a tempest is creating havoc for the Night Palace. Oceans must have originated from the melting of comets in deluges of rain. One of these days, they will send their waves far outside the solar system.

The imagination seeks through the sea's lethargy Being's mysterious borders, as if Being were an enchanted lake. Says the Iliad, "on the divine sea they're launching a black vessel!"

The Final Judgment occurs uninterruptedly, like the sea. They define each other.

And there's something beyond time about these wars, this water. No question has been raised about the mind's suspension within the universe's suspension. No object moving. No subject watching. A mobility of another order. Mutability.

Fire and water. A resurgent Minotaur is howling in the depth of the night.

It's scary. The storm is hissing. Waves are brutal. The wind is whistling and the cold is lonely. Everything is apocalyptic.

F O G

to Brandon Shimoda

Waking in the countryside, element of one's memory, one feels the spirit's weight. Still, the night sky. We travelers breathe an archaic fire's residue.

In obscurity, visions quiet the mind. We're on an ocean superimposed on the incommensurable Pacific. Air and soul, interchangeable.

Destructive forces gather momentum in unchartered territories. There's a saturation of dreams from which one doesn't awake; it's like living in mirrors. It's not color that I see, but I see.

The spirit is diluted in this low-altitude. Be careful when stepping on anything that is not at one with itself. Speaking to one's shadow is part of the morning exercise. To be on the way to an outer-world, to get used to uselessness.

The fog is starting to crawl over the waters. Oh to be on this Earth! Ocean steaming. And what's brewing in the heart? What's dissolving, if not one's mind? The divine resides at the hills' bottom, not in the valley.

Heat accumulates on the sea and we're as naked as the landscape. The fog's skin bears no marks. Empirical reality submits to mist, drugs, sleep... attracts lines, shapes, dimensions or noise; lower temperatures, too.

At certain hours sunlight falls in oblique lines. Self-awareness consumes much power. You can say that you're a container of cities. There's a tempest with no wind. Crowns of gold are drawn to peripheries.

Music, as an expression of splendor, lasted all night long. New tensions sustain cosmic phenomena. We all become "deities," like matter has already.

Do we pursue darkness because daylight means exhaustion? Being unveiled is being impoverished. We're not returning to Dionysus but to his double's residence. Dionysus waiting to be born.

Obscurity is separation from light. A white, aerial beast keeps descending – Yosemite Falls. We watch the brain drying. A green leaf has fallen from the apple tree. Thirst for the animals. A lone meteor changing its course.

To descend on language the way obscurity descends on a city. Night speaks. Being is active, made desperate by its own intensity, violent. Language is that essential violence.

In its impatience to borrow clouds, night bursts into day. That event is outrageous. There's not an eclipse, though, in this moment, just our intrusion into alien territory.

Liszt, Cosima, Wagner – lives spent as a succession of storms – now gone. Since, rose bushes fade rapidly. A stream is shining under the shadows!

Something impalpable has seduced the gods, but they're slowly dissolving. We look for their traces, wonder about the meaning of divine destiny. We're led by the memory of a mountain that was, once, a state of mind.

I have to deal with a particular danger that aims at annihilating the world, appearance to appearance.

The wind has the orgiastic power to displace summer heat and overgrown trees. Time is running faster than trains. Deep canyons reverberate the brain's grooves. Death is a running away from the present.

Rivers run to where people from different geometries wait. The moon's indecision turns this place into a morph. Remembering Heidegger's abruptness. His archeological mind. A dark word, his.

Hail is disrupting the day. Shattered peace. For the fog, a fur coat. There's melancholy at this hour.

To think without the world, is that possible? Is thinking more material than we know? There are affinities that escape our perception: the unknown is an immense reality.

Nothingness is more reassuring than a cluttered paradise. In Time's magnitude there's no room for passion. We need to hang on the idea of the non return.

The weather doesn't interfere with receding waves. Series of lightning circle the night sky. At last, an epic wind. The ground is shaking in all innocence.

No hand is going to raise the curtain, not mine. Two shots have been heard in the silky night. Rabbits pricked up their ears. Emptiness is an unverifiable concept.

And the trees are frozen even though immobility is fiction. The soil is hypnotized by the red needles that are covering it. The Minotaur is probably in the Rain Forest, out from the Labyrinth. He's probably sobbing.

All kinds of diseases inhabit our solitude. Some people witness their soul's death before dying. That's an apocalyptic event, a private eclipse.

To close one's eyes is to create one thousand fogs. The night after the Crucifixion was longer than usual. There are people still living in it, as if nothing happened since.

The brain's substance is bleeding out through a pipe fixed at one of its corners. We die of the same kind of death as a fly's. How can an idea travel faster than light and leave us behind?

Heraclitus had a clear sight: no one, nothing created the sun. Something always was, and will be. Circular or horizontal, how to tell? Did he figure out that we would become intergalactic? Tonight clouds are on an outing. Away from the ocean's barbaric appeal.

The living do contemplate the dead. What about death's absolute dominion?

Possibilities are demanding. Under an unforgiving glare cactuses give birth to fragile flowers: an unsustainable beauty. Oh to envision Mount Olympus!

Are dreams well lit? Opinions differ. Once in a while against a black background a figure moves... A let down follows. Pain. Has anyone experienced a fog that would be warm? Such insolence if it were to be.

Excess of life. Ants deconstructing their shelters. It's raining unto the bones.

At a lunar cycle's end Minotaur appears. He's loose, he's tall. No nervous system resists his onslaught. How primitive appears the sea when, like a butterfly wing, like a heart, the sun lifts itself from a trail of fog. As primitive as the wild beast.

Being, awesome, even in its gentleness. Ocean of sounds. Waves beating against shore. Universe enlarging, but within what? The container expends ad infinitum. A hat is always larger than a head.

The mind pursues strange and wasted objects... a shifting, an exchange. Diffident was love, difficult, disabled. Where flowers won't, time will grow, will sail through the world's thickness.

Birds are disoriented by the sun's sudden absence. People too. Between body and thought there's no place for a thread, and still, such a distance. The waters will never compete with the mind's persistence.

Full moon over the buildings. Generations gone. Shadows will proceed on white paper. Eyelashes create shadows too, on a face's paleness. We favor the ephemeral over the stable.

On the land of ancient Syria a young man has been buried – a political prisoner, a hero – in these non-heroic times. A dead man's isolation is of another nature than ours'. Implacable. We're the victims of the theology of power.

We're seeking no relief but something akin to it when we're in front of a coffin containing a dead body. Somebody who was alive is starting to rot. Not perspiring anymore. Sealed in total darkness. Sealed.

To be in the fog is to be in a state of suspension. What's true is then not true; the mind's liberation. Beyond anti-matter, more matter or more spirit?

When we say that nothing will survive, we affirm nothingness' eminence. Its centrality. A box takes center stage. Stays there.

Myriads of wrinkles make up the sea's surface. On high mountains we find crevasses that spit those water springs that eventually become the rivers that make History start.

Linden trees wear crowns of blossoms in Brandon Shimoda's garden. Mount Fuji today in tears. Mount Rainier scowling. It's always late afternoon, with always fog in the eyes. We loved an Apollonian deity in the days of our eternity.

The soul's dark summits are not negotiable. Io is turning around Prometheus as I'm turning around a fire which burns the way water runs.

When all space is filled with a monstrous fog that jumps off the horizon, my different personae are shed. A translucent body is left, and Time unfolds as supreme enemy.

But that space is also an epiphany.

Disasters imply a misconception of reality. The heart is a stranger to the patterns of matter or their distribution. In darkness, light's new measure.

It's the Night Palace that's floating on this overwhelming disaster; it doesn't define the sunset but rather vanishes with it. We were at Dostoievsky's funeral. The coffin was kept open long before the burial. Before the end.

But the letters that write his name are in a perpetual consumption. The ensuing heat is what we call life: a combustion. Nothingness' return is not its recurrence, because in this case there's no interruption.

The "whole" is familiar with itself, given its impermanence, and probably its non-existence.

We yearn for the void in the here and now. Billions of gallons of water rest on the moon, a dangerous incentive for the human race to discard planet Earth and break loose. Those who will not make the voyage will find their condition unbearable.

Dostoievsky is visiting: hidden by a veil woven by Ibn 'Arabi. The two haven't died, though not because we think of them or that they're immortal. Dostoievsky is looking for a patch of land in Russia to start a forest.

Meanwhile, September fires have resumed. The brain remains cool, monitoring its survival. Its fragmentation would be an avatar of darkness, its dusk. The fog has arrived, un-cluttering the air. It's so light and still so total. Its smoothness has no borders.

.

Snakes open the path to death. Let winter enter the room to tell us why the sea is high. The sea is breathing, splashing, unconcerned. But a heart is fainting. The brain's hemispheres are receiving different lights; in this silence.

What does it mean to belong to a land? For those of us who live away from our private history, the question never heals.

The fog's project is to unsubstantiate reality. Mountains occupy inadvertently one's complete consciousness. The sea retires into the distance. Resurrection doesn't necessarily mean paradise.

There, near the retrieved Night Palace, the foghorn. The storm has resumed. A train has emerged from its tunnel to enter a woman's womb through a line of autumn trees.

Old American nut trees turn into Indian spirits. Love precedes us to the grave and follows us into it. A stream. The season's melancholy bores holes into the soul.

Sometimes, memories of a Pacific beach weigh as much as a killer wave.

Thinking moves on its own horizon, with its own fuel. It swings between its attraction to the world and its own laws. Oneness with the one. An influx of birds passing over the river.

We're flooded by incurable energies. There's no way out of one's skin, one's language, one's passions. Will Being's collapse happen in this universe or in another?

Writing is an activity that confronts images with the ideas that try to sort them out. But when fires begin to engulf big chunks of California, we turn numb.

Some 400 planets are orbiting around stars outside the solar system. There are also intermediary zones, chasms, where life throbs, like in this room, this fog.

Thoughts have color. The blue ones, the blues. Rust-colored meditations on the sunset, numbers with a yellow tinge. They have scents too.

Within every poet's belly lies a pulsating sense of loss. A loss. We live in the midst of apprehensions. The countryside is ablaze and the shadows, willingly transparent.

The weather's dullness affects the physical heart. One waits to hear the clouds over the San Francisco hills, their steady strides. To swim in air!

If it doesn't rain on the moon how are they going to plant flowers over there?

Nothing exists save this inner luminosity that needs to transform space into moving steam. My angels are not yours.

Wind is a god enticing us into disbelief. After a season of brightness, one of non-visibility. In the fog the body's immateriality.

One can't think without remembering. Rains pour on language too. O fever! O weather!

The brain wonders why the mind is constantly drifting, and the latter asks itself why it has to be oozing from a soft, gelatinous mass, so thoroughly imprisoned in utter blackness.

Fog operates like a drug: its presence means bliss; its absence is addiction not satisfied, a dreadful withdrawal.

Landscape produces infinite *tristesse*.

Being enthroned. One believes to be walking in a forest while descending to a private hell. This question: "Did you, like me, die when you lost me?

Ecriture is no different from planting roses. Bombs are relentlessly being dropped. To go to war is to enhance one's life at the detriment of other lives. We can't easily abandon such pleasures.

The elusive 'now' is just the present's intensity. When in disarray we realize how relative reality can be; we hear music made with no instruments, we traverse books.

Light decreases without changing its speed. Every object is linked to the past: this chair, this mountain. Then, what about this idea?

Once more, only in darkness, light.

Unlit rooms filled with loss; to what do they lead? Beatitude with a negative sign, there, where adolescent love keeps haunting.

A fractured skull lies on the sidewalk, a victim of imperial power. Civilization is built on the ability to corrupt. Nietzsche is perfect innocence; independent from human nature, a sailboat. The ocean, his equal.

Thinking starts at a beginning, like the source of the Rhine in Hölderlin's poem.

The deer that angels allowed to come close to the house laid under the pine trees and barely moved their eyelashes, their legs. There, the Angel of the Last Instant failed to appear.

Soldiers in their tanks took shelter under olive trees. Night was not going to be late. Earth was trembling. The soldiers and the deer slept, each thinking that everything is what it has to be.

A head is none other than a deformed planet. How can one know what it contains when its owner doesn't? But it does contain the "I" anyway. A face, when looked at seriously, is terrifying. Still, faces fill the streets.

A poem is an atom. Better to leave it alone. Who needs more nuclear explosions!

We inhabit a terror we call life. With burned fingers we pick up signs on the floors of forests. At undue hours, we study anatomy. The mind is its own construct. Therefore what?

We write in silence. Something faints on each page. How to apprehend any person? How to make sure that seeing anything is not seeing oneself? How to forego one's self without losing that miserable self? What would perpetual revelation be?

A gathering of necessities?

Being is just a horizon. It's thinkable but we're not able to think it: that's what is meant by "living in obscurity." We face the river and know intimately how it feels to be that kind of running water. A river is a river: that's obscurity too, but also a key to canyons, to estuaries.

Right now the millennium's longest eclipse is happening over a land stretching from Kenya to China. It will last 11 minutes, 8 seconds.

Memory has large avenues where cars surge with their headlights on. Strident sounds. Effervescence.

A pallid reflection of one thought on another creates chaos. Why not? Inappropriate behavior brings devastation on this cruel part of the world. The fog enters in the cupboards, drawers, limbs and ears: they disappear for a while, we breathe better.

Whoever loved a person the way he loved a river has lost both: that's called a natural disaster.

We're looking at a galaxy 28 billion years away, so says Hubble. The archaic is as far away as the future, with us in between.

Desire brings out differences. Nature appears so remote when not angry. We're surrounded by things absent, like a particular valley down by a mountain-range. There's much malady on this shrinking planet. Fog moving on the mind.

The universe is more lonesome than we are. It goes to sleep on abandoned meadows, deserted grounds. This night is poor.

There's a lingering light. Gulls are sitting on the fence, speaking about the great difficulties they experienced on their route.

The blue moon's beauty is pantheistic.

The sun rises and eats a chunk of the Kilimanjaro. Then it continues its way and the chunk returns. By mid-afternoon, the fog makes the mountain go.

How to know if memory isn't spatial? A house seen with closed eyes is always warped. After their manifestation, things need to recede unto themselves.

Rivers, mountains, oceans, all involved in power struggles. Earth is a cemetery, until the next sentence, and the next glass of wine.

Underground trains create impersonal journeys. Who will tell the last story, and to whom? A box containing a dead body keeps the world away. Drift.

The progression of the days is irrevocable.

When the mind stares at itself what does it see? A vanishing blur? The inner demon's return?

Every moment a starting point, thinking on the move, traveling. Is thinking pandemic?

The universe could have taken myriads of roads other than the one it took; it's exiled too. "Indigo horizon pure whole unbroken sight seeing it," thinks, says and writes Leslie Scalapino, a cup of coffee in her hand.

Not seeing rivers is also another way of dying. Hours are lining up in cinematic motion.

Plants are eager to break rank. The sage and the verbena have grown taller than the rest. Patients are scared, dreaming to escape.

Trees are imitating the government by always bending under the slightest pressure. We're prisoners of the concept of disaster.

The pubs have closed. The alleys are impracticable. A stream by the road, singing, a streetlight fading in the fog. Mind staggers over its productions. Ideas, foggy, love, impossible.

All there's left to do is to listen, over the radio, to a baseball game. We have ran out of taboos. Killing has become a big bore.

Birds fly in the great emptiness which is their heart's repetitive desert. Skies, waves on waves move directly into one's head. An eclipse can bring illumination to the soul.

After the debilitating ecstasy, the twilight. Sirens are sending warnings against an impending flooding. Let's stay within the coming night.

All the light bulbs are in position, and functioning. There's nothing special to report. At least for a while, Earth will remain a planet.

Does this cold body collaborate with the pain it feels, or is it obliged to bear it?

The beauty experienced was an illusion. All it did was accelerate that particular heartbeat that records our fall.

Cold + cold is an algebraic equation: the snow's whiteness traps the line of blood that's running through life's fire.

To turn over in one's bed is often like changing hemispheres. We reached the possibility of immanence but it's not sure that the species will transcend itself.

The lassitude will linger, in the body. in the weather. The weather is the lover. A whole range of red mountains is lit by the sinking sun, and has become an immense electro-magnetic system.

You and I met on the day of Creation. The cataclysm is still in us. We may come back as grass, be eaten. A trail will remain, a path, the next storm.

A fog, massive, sumptuous, is stronger than the passage of a thousand angels. Recurring.

Love burns like coals in a long stormy night.

Grass grows short of flying. The roots' resilience, the pressure. Adding days on days.

Living on the moon may well turn out to be worse than being where we were, an emptiness with no future.

Here, we hear the future knocking on the windows. That's not a thing to be dismissed.

In sadness there's more energy than in this affirmative existence. This routine.

A ghost arrived with a handful of roses. "No other flower is a flower," he said. He left them on a table and quit; the more the place darkened, the more they glowed.

A smell of iodine pervades the sea. Salt in the air. The past drifting with the breeze. The faraway Sierra Nevada is giving signs of restlessness, and the coastline is shifting aimlessly.

The desert is an open uranium pit. Deliriums mushrooming. You will contemplate death, says the Book of Revelation.

Is making love mentally to a dead lover making love to death? Does it come from the desire to rupture time and create a chasm into which one will fall and find the lover intact, although not breathing?

Then, at a certain hour, everything will smooth out. The horizon moves forward in softness then fades. In the process we lose our way to a dream.

Rupture of one's veins. Blood flowing "inland." Death's meaning revealed as lack of shelter, of light.

Love: cosmic absolute black center radiating...

Girls who witnessed the mother's suicide never trust the world. No man will later attract them, no woman will keep them. Once in a while they will establish with the night secret relations that no one else could ever imagine.

I'm listening to something that wasn't meant to be heard...

Measuring light's intensity is akin to figuring out an ancient Hopi's attraction to his habitat. We cover trees with crowns, and try to convince mountains that they are sacred Indian chiefs. The Colorado River has stories to tell.

The fog is licking the ground and stretching over the hills. Slowly, crawling higher. Picking up light at its edges. Moving. Nature not keeping archives.

I want the glaciers of the highest mountains to share my miseries. I want a sudden spring.

To be is to have been and intending to be. It's not dissimilar to driving a car. Everything we do is in analogy with what we are.

To take pleasure in the void is an operation of erasure, a denial of the ocean's power, or one's preparation for the time when ocean will engulf all that there is.

A sky without a single cloud isn't necessarily blue – it can be sheer light. We wish not to disappear before having had at least one illumination. But illumination is like that sky, with no shadows, no mercy.

So what about fog? Total fog is total illumination. We're driving with no visibility down a winding and steep hill, toward army barracks, then to the ocean. It's not sure we will make it. But the fascination is fatal. It's fused with the world.

Poetry is metaphysical. We're searching for ways to see, to arrest, to tell, in the great passion for the eternal flow.

And eternity may disappear too.

So mind has its own black holes that swallow tumultuous rivers, mountain ranges, galaxies, as well as toys, trees and memories... we have to follow the weather.

Muddy lakes are swelling across the sky.

From what appears to what's hidden and from what's hidden to what appears: always on the road.

The storm withdrew after closing the door. On which side of the door were we? The question is: can fire be controlled?

The sea has taken measure of her nature. She's a flat mercurial metal today, as she was yesterday. Herself a sign.

When you walked the deserts of the Andes amid their lakes of salt you searched for fresh water. The possibility of losing your mind left you then indifferent.

In certain areas of the world countries are made to explode by remote-control. It used to be said "by divine will." It was easier to resist God's decisions than today's super-powers.

It's because God moved within Himself that He let the world be. Where does this lead us to? To the need of a God that doesn't die? But Nature moves the world and dies without dying and includes us in all its processes.

How to find the road that rises gently toward its own horizon so that the sky touches the earth with no physical contact and no commotion? How to reach that stage where to know anything would be superfluous?

Though thinking is inseparable from life, how wonderful to have it suspended, neutralized, not in a kind of sleep but in the most acute form of awareness.

When the sun goes down, a chill descends with it, and spreads. Sometimes gas from one star hits another star's surface and undergoes nuclear fusion.

There's no use telling that absence is heart of existence when someone dies. The dead don't come back the way we knew them and no divinity – even when out of its season - has ever done anything to make things different from what they are.

I opened the drawer and freed a bunch of flowers. My eyes followed their journey to the top of a hearse, and saw the fog leap over the Bridge – there was nothing to be seen over the ocean, not even the ocean.

Earth is wandering. Moon's round eye dreaming. The fields are on fire. We're entering the heart of strangeness.

Thinking helps the flowering of the body... the sun attracts it, then when there's a drought on the land, a mortal accident... thinking dies.

The red sun is taking possession of Brittany's pink granite.

My fever burned for a hundred years over the lands of an unnamed planet bigger than this one.

In Europe's narrow streets young men do not anymore harbor dreams of conquests.

In pain, even. A thin gray and luminous ribbon cuts through a canyon. Then its flow increases; it's now a torrent. The mist is boiling. The temperature has fallen.

There's a moment to the moment. We're in the world.

We fear violence, but more feared is its absence. So heavy is the world becoming. Heavy in the soul. A few laps in the ocean will bring rest.

There's what I will erase, and what will be erased, this chestnut tree that will disappear, that fog that's already melting into air, and surely this planet, and further what's not yet discovered, everything on its way out...

If only thinking could get as impenetrable as darkness, wash off what it pretends to know, die to itself, and land somewhere with no space nor time, as pure presence...

Verbs are not agreeable to Being because the latter enjoys its seclusion. Hypnotized, we free ourselves by shifting our energies on different matters, unless, like Cézanne – and only Cézanne – we paint apples ad infinitum.

As an answer to stagnation we demolish; for lack of love, we take the car on an outing, and not believing, we speak of religion..

There's no dissolution of space, it seems. But we die. No explanation makes sense. Darkness doesn't cover what's not there.

So spring's vitality will be contagious, at least for a while. We have not created the seasons, but they rule the numbers by which we live.

We fear love, supreme terror lying at truth's deepest layer.

Like an onion that you peel ring after ring, ending on a void, your "identity" turns around a hole... but if a tree is, I am, – for each, a destiny.

Transparencies within obscurity: in objects, empty space, or ideas. Sometimes we break their inner walls to uncover their mystery, but to remain in the dark.

When everything alive will have disappeared, the great expanses of sheer rock under a pitiless sun will start to show that they too have an inner life

They administered electro-shocks to the poet. They could as well have beaten his brain with baseball bats. They reduced him to a haggard and confused wounded tiger. We used to go from café to café in search of him. Whenever we found him, we gave him cigarettes.

Poetry had already burned his brain, but differently. It had enlarged his pupils. Though reading his works aloud in the streets, we were ill at-ease as we had a little money, and he had none.

In the Orion nebula the Herschel special observatory revealed the imprints of organic molecules such as water, carbon monoxide, hydrogen, cyanide, methanol... O impatience!

We're sliding inexorably toward a new rapport with Nature: would the trip to Mars alter the way we shoot birds?

The rosebush in the remaining garden will remain equal to itself, but would our sense of smell respond?

Still, we're going into the deep sky. We monitor hydrogen's particular radiation when heated by the birth of new stars and detect photons escaping and being intercepted by clouds of interstellar gas and dust. We're getting ready.

In the mean-time empires are crumbling. Earth has become too small for the energies that are being unleashed. As revolutions have lost their appeal, mega-storms are in the making, involving weather, matter, and destruction.

Better to stay in the shade, where memory weakens more easily. Better even to stay awake till the early hours of the day so to have the luxury of refusing the light.

It rains. It rains. Visibility is decreasing. It's raining stones. The sun is lying in the vicinity of the horizon. We're probably walking on its rays. The times are demanding attention. People are staying in.

Having walked miles in thick fog I ran into the most luminous vision of a new kind of darkness in which the mind resides uninterruptedly and from which it proceeds. (Water starting a river).

The pursuit of the surrounding fog may well be the pursuit of the mother.

Walking now on a dirt road: there's some grass, here and there. Patches of snow, far from each other. The ground is reddish. Some thorns. Stones all over. Lines of small bushes. We're in Death Valley.

In the yard, a tree is showing the first leaves of the season. I feel neither related, nor a stranger. Just looking.

We need the world's wildness – without which we'll be mud.

Today, in the coldest place in the universe, (a couple of degrees above absolute zero), 2 beams of protons collided at CERN, Geneva. They approached, at a tiny scale, what happened in the first split seconds after the Big Bang.

How can one, under a splendid sun, and with intimate news about the universe, be desperate?

On one hand, yourself, only your self. On the other, the ocean, immense, given to itself, and probably to you.

Pergolesi's *Salve Regina*

In all innocence the fog is touching the tip of the trees. The forest is silent. It doesn't mind its invasion by such a light substance. Lighter than a dance, than a hand.

This stepping out into the fog – this sudden coolness on the face, this diffused environment ... the body responds, then lets go.

The sum total of all human sufferings is civilization too.

Away from the ecstatic zone, it's not rain or fog that falls on their eyes, but blood. To each his/her tormentor, to each his/her victim.

A rainbow is making a shield between me and my thoughts.

Au fur et à mesure

We're left with a panic fear. If we had wings we would have flown, but airplanes have become versions of the living-room. The dying-room.

Regularly, only the fog can change the world.

But the fog is cruel. Its sponginess absorbs one's inattentiveness. Stepping out from the Night Palace, Joanne Kyger comes face to face with the Pacific's depth in that obscure journey.

Into that fog and not to "where and what." Any life is too short to matter. Earth sweats humid air. We're summoning bits of love in order to float in this weather-event whose silvery substance engulfs San Francisco regularly...

Prisoner of his wife's madness, a man remains in his room until daylight comes to hurt his eyes. Later, heavy masses of fog move over a beginning sunset.

If you're willing to reach the divine through memory's workings – go through that fog. Let time run its course. Listen. If nothing happens, it would mean that you reached the invisible.

My eyes liberate a flat and moving surface that wants to travel along my decisions.

I say the sea is overwhelmed by its waves. Breathe into it your thoughts, and it will remember you.

Death and life are similar in so far that they're each a thin layer that hides the incomprehensible.

Would mind dominate Being where gods failed?

Invisibility reigns supreme. Why do we ignore the reality of the given and need to look behind it?

Archeology is the recurrence of the past into the present. We didn't leave the gods, they did us.

There's no tension in a late sleep on the beach. The world penetrates the lungs and elevates the mind to the only rest it can experience.

In the meantime, the waters beat against an alien construction and the heat invades the city.

The forest spreads its thickness on a map. Entering head-on to where each tree has a shadow is to enter the future.

A forest is equally a little universe of solitude where one's impulses grow as tall as the trees, but also are as imprisoned in immobility.

When time is new and over here an-ill fated tide advances on the mind... tomorrow has nothing to do with what preceded it.

We spend a life-time running after our life, running into that soft wall, looking for the energy to die.

But sometimes we're distracted ... we're visited by Nature's own doings, by her capacity to absorb our will, to give us oblivion.

I am immortal not because I have been, but because I am.

The sea is beating like a heart, heading into a sloppy moisture. At this encounter's frontier, a turbulence from outer-space asks to participate.

I would – as I usually do in June and July, when the weather is warm, and deeper California hot – come to the Pacific shore to join the cosmic fog-event in its transfiguration.

A steady fog has sent fishermen to harbor, coastal birds into hiding, the foghorn, to silence.

To be trapped in the fog is different from being lost in a forest. Breathing is most concerned.

We are the world reflecting on itself, a medium, exalted, discarded.

Love enters the arteries and speeds up the heart.

Only in the fog do I feel complete.

Time and fog escape our grasp. But when I drive through a visiting cloud, though limited to a (blissful) moment, I negotiate directly with a cosmic happening, I domesticate an impersonal part of Nature.

Time is my country, fog is my land.

Come along, my
   fog, foggy
   sky,
      sky not disappeared,
         (and fog),
      because
         of foghorns

O angelic
   figure once
   beloved
– not even
   dust today,
do not fear
   this morning,
   where I
   awoke

Come along
  this road
  gentle wind
be careful,
  the years
  have
  gone

Listen, spirit,
  ocean, friends
have left
  for where there's
  no space,
  no scratches,
a window
  left alone

Don't worry
  my love
fog is no
  sign, no
  message,
just a passing
  cloud

Nobody is coming
this night of
obscurity

The hill is descending
into that
night
as slowly
as ever

We forgot the
warning,
soft grass
underfoot,
and fear,
always fear

Days move
   like we do,
      they're thrown away
   down here
where we live

Sweet angels take
   us by the hand
      when we walk
   to the beach,
      the beach mesmerizes

Allow me o God
   in whom I don't
      believe
to finish this
   line, this
      early evening

I return to the
  fog because
    it is
      me,
it has a magnitude
    that humans
      lack,
it covers
    spaces

How lonely
  can one
    become,
thinner than
  a dream,
as planted
  as a
    tree

Blood is
　　no perfume
but in some
　　cities it
　　　flows freely

Yes, the fog
　　is ominous,
faithful
　　companion,
　　　unifier of
　　concepts

Movies live
　　fast,
　　　they end, then
　　　return,
we are a
　　screen,
nothing else

A year of railroad
  tracks,
    of earthquakes,
the will is tired

Death moves in
  like a soft
    wind
  between
    layers
  of dread

You hover above
  my impoverished
    nudity
but we can't return
  to where we
    started

In a city stressed
by the light
unredeemable,
a lover
weighs,
on the body,
on memory

The sea is not
deep enough to
contain the hour
that just went
unnoticed

we are undone by
beauty's effect on
the arteries,
its carnivorous
essence,
its solitude

my soul,
  nights are long when you're
    sleepless,
forget that you
  inhabit my limbs,
try to
    survive

Don't worry,
  sit down, my
  soul,
I'll close the
  door

Fear me not,
  I may leave you
soon,
  which of us will descend
    first into
      hell?
we're at a loss

The fog has entered
  my nostrils
in this blind street

Not a single leaf
  is left over my heart to
    be peeled off,
everything is
  expendable

Devastating for the
  spirit, always,
    is the next wave

Let the fog in,
  the one coming from you
    and
covering
ˋ my soul
with your substance,
  your destiny

Sit in front
  of me, sit,
we're used to seeing
  through the
    dark

in the nights of
  her absence
my body
  was waiting,
    for her
      soul

We knew fog over
  matter,
in stupefaction,
  my body was at odds
    with yours,
breaking down

We can't make up
   for lost time
how can we?
   you're no more

This thing that I am
   – dear soul –
will decompose,
   we know,
where would you go
   then?
happiness came from it,
   not from
   divinities

There's malady in
   the air
the waters are temporarily
      exalting
         the
         world

The coffin went
   down
the alley,
   death is simply the
    end of
     meaning

As my body thinks
   painfully
what's left for you,
if not this love,
so ancient in
   difficulty,
    o why?

I want to take you,
   my soul,
   to the
largest rivers

listen – think
how fast that
river
was

the rock is
granite
heated,
cut,
gasping for
air

lines of cockroaches
leaving the basement
for our beds

the father holding
a burning
rod
teaching
punishment

The fog is
  moving in with
    force

Her body will not
  return to mine
and I will not return

The multiplicity of
  the love and the lie
has been
    the knife of
      my undoing,
pieces,
    distributed
      along the road

It rains on my
  brain
fear has settled

O my soul, am
   I you?
 when I'm talking to you
   it's because I think you
     will listen,
 knowing you might not...

but the involvement with
     you is
     fatal

every window thinks of
   itself as being an
     opening

ISBN: 978-0-9844598-7-2

Design and typesetting by HR Hegnauer
Cover painting by Etel Adnan
Text set in Adobe Garamond Pro

Cataloging-in-publication data is available
From the Library of Congress

Nightboat Books
Callicoon, New York
www.nightboat.org

Nightboat Books

Nightboat Books, a nonprofit organization, seeks to develop audiences for writers whose work resists convention and transcends boundaries. We publish books rich with poignancy, intelligence, and risk. Please visit our website, www.nightboat.org, to learn about our titles and how you can support our future publications.

This book was made possible by a grant from the Topanga Fund, which is dedicated to promoting the arts and literature of California.

The following individuals have supported the publication of this book. We thank them for their generosity and commitment to the mission of Nightboat Books:

Kazim Ali
Anonymous
Elizabeth Motika
Benjamin Taylor

This book has been made possible, in part, by a grant from the New York State Council on the Arts Literature Program.

State of the Arts

NYSCA